Law oτ

Purpose.

Law of Purpose.

Series "Laws of the Universe "
By: Sherry Lee
Version 1.1 ~August 2023
Published by Sherry Lee at KDP
Copyright ©2023 by Sherry Lee. All rights reserved.

3

TABLE OF CONTENTS.

INTRODUCTION.

Dharma is your life's purpose. Each person is unique, and when we lose track of time while experiencing pleasure, harmony, exultation, and timelessness, we know we are contributing by following our respective talents. We are here to assist one another. When we inquire, "How can I give?" We engage in a spiritual dialogue and receive a response from the creative source.

Your purpose is whatever you assign it. God/Source/Creator gave us a talent, however. Using our expertise will achieve two significant outcomes:

It will bring us great happiness,

It will enable us to contribute more to society than any other acquired skill.

There are many ways to discover your purpose in life, but if you are on the correct path, you will be happy, and others will value your work. They will value your work in words and deeds and monetary compensation.

It makes no difference if you are an artist, businessperson, or barrister. If you respect your unique abilities, you will be successful and content. Typically, these emotions have a positive effect on self-esteem.

However, your self-esteem may suffer if your family is critical and believes everyone must be a lawyer and you are the only non-lawyer. However, it will not suffer as much if you yield and become a lawyer.

The world is full of attorneys who would rather be farmers or farmers who would rather be bridge-building engineers, or physicians who would rather be police officers. Please, please, please, don't become one of these miserable individuals who will remain miserable until they recognize their talents.

CHAPTER 1: THE LAW OF PURPOSE OR DHARMA.

Each moment is a thought, and as thoughts, they swiftly pass into oblivion and are lost forever. Our mind stores a reference snapshot of the moment's fervor and labels it with emotion to continue tormenting us in the future. However, it is genuinely gone forever.

Our mind groups these instances so that we can perceive a complete narrative, but this is not the Truth of the moment. This is comparable to a film passing through a projector, with each frame creating the illusion of motion and actuality. It is not genuine; it is neither Action nor Life. Although you are immersed in the illusion of living in the film for a moment, it has nothing to do with you.

Observe your thoughts as they come and go, leading you to the next preposterous notion. Within a minute, the final thought in this line is unrelated to the preceding one. That is the Mind's Consciousness Stream.

This linear logic is advantageous for human survival. It keeps the animal alive and improves our ability to function in this dimension. Others can comprehend our logical language. We can all generally refer to a tree as a "Tree" and a red object as a "Red Object," We can all find acceptable definitions for each.

However, everything can be broken down into its component elements, atoms, a single moment or thought, or a celluloid frame. The tree consists of bark, foliage, fiber, and sap. Similar to the film, Tree is a synthesis of fundamental ideas. We observe a tree because we define the combined elements as a tree.

Similarly, a "scene" from your life can be broken down into component moments or thoughts. (Everything Is Thought). Each thought arises, and we perceive it with our senses or on the movie screen of our mind. The mind then connects a few concepts, keeps the projector running, and creates a linear understanding of the scene.

We do this often. Psychologists have demonstrated that if a person is given a jumbled, random assortment of sounds or film segments, they will attempt to organize them and develop an emotional attachment to the story they create.

We are experts at this! Our mind's primary function is to create a scene and make us comprehend it. You have a moment, followed by another, then another. Your reasoning connects them to construct a short story. Nonetheless, each moment - each frame of film - is fleeting. This is the Law of universal change. The moment passed, for better or worse, and it was impossible to halt.

This should relieve you, as life is filled with wonderful and horrifying events. Both will inevitably pass. You can live a happy existence by remembering the good times and rejecting the negative ones when they arise.

Even scenes you fear, such as flying in an airplane, will fade away moment by moment.

So, what do you do with these Moments flowing through your mind?

Live each moment wholeheartedly. Don't allow your mind to worry about the next moment; it will come, and if you live it to the fullest when it appears, you will have done well! That is ALL that is possible in existence.

- Live Presently.

- Live each moment to the fullest.

- Live in the NOW.

Your mind causes you to anticipate (stress about) the next moment or to relive the past. The future and the past don't exist; they are nonexistent.

How many beautiful flowers do you walk past daily while fretting about something that may never occur?

How many precious moments with your infant have you missed because you were preoccupied with something else?

Will he ever again be a child?

If you lived each moment at work to the fullest and gave each task your undivided attention, you would have undoubtedly reached the pinnacle by now. Then, at 6:00 p.m., you can depart the office and devote yourself to your family and friends.

It is known as Mindfulness.

Giving your Life to the Present; making the present your entire life.

Remember that the mind is constantly working to maintain the illusion of this world (samsara), without which you (ego) would cease to exist. It's a form of survival.

Since the world is thought, the mind's primary function is to build the world and You within it. To keep you engaged in the world it creates, the mind clings ceaselessly to your attention and interests, generating dramas, anxieties, and desires.

Quite literally, you Are Your Mind! All of the world's definitions, including all definitions of SELF, are generated by this immense Supercomputer of Consciousness!

This is the film you inhabit. You are attentive to all mental dramas. You constantly seek more action and drama while ignoring what is closest to our conception of Reality. You disregard the Present. Zen Masters say, "When walking, walk. When seated, just sit". Just exist in the present. This moment is the only reality that exists.

CHAPTER 2: WHAT IS THE PURPOSE OF YOUR LIFE?

The purpose of life is to be joyous. That which you are, life force energy, is inherently love, well-being, eagerness, exhilaration, and happiness. According to your statisticians, this is your "baseline" as you enter the world. When you incarnate, your soul has no original transgression or karmic stain. You arrive on earth fresh, clean, and eager for another adventure!

Pollution and other environmental toxins can wreak havoc on your health, and the world's system is set up for the benefit of elites while most people struggle. Many earthly belief systems are self-limiting; you construct your lives and societies based on their contents.

For example, the belief that "there is only so much to go around" is among the most limiting beliefs on your planet. It has caused many of the evils you detest. We inform you that a shift in thought can change the physical principles that your scientists consider absolute.

Changes in mindset, such as "energy must come from scarce fossil fuels" to "we can discover (or create) the laws of nature that allow us to extract clean, abundant energy from the environment," must inevitably result in a complete shift in how and where energy is gotten. If everyone had ample vitality, the war would be unnecessary! Conflicts are waged over limited resources.

Much of the history of your planet consists of the deliberate construction of scarcity and the ensuing rise of hierarchical societies to reflect this belief. Such beliefs can only thrive if they are widely or fervently held. We inform you that thought power is transcendent.

We wish for all your readers to ponder, "What is my life's purpose?" Many of you will respond, "I don't know."

Can you articulate your life's purpose in one or two concise sentences?

How else could you create your life?

What would a house without a coherent blueprint appear like?

The situation would resemble a Three Stooges farce!

Before having a life purpose, one must have a desire. This is repeated often because it is so essential.

Every purpose commences with a desire. Based on this desire, purpose and intent can materialize. As with a house's blueprint, you can construct a prototype of thought that will guide your actions and attract the people and resources you require.

Without this plan, your existence will appear to be a series of random occurrences. Either that or you will repeatedly encounter similar situations because you must consciously give yourself direction.

The most important work you will ever perform is identifying a desire and imagining how you want your life to appear. It amazes us that so few of you consciously take the time to perform this labor. It is the most satisfying and enjoyable labor you will ever perform!

However, if you examine the lives of these individuals, you will find that each of them had a distinct purpose in mind. It would be best to establish your vibrational resonance by determining what you want before allowing the universe to bring it to you.

Along the route, you generate creative ideas, which you then implement. We assure you that this formula will inevitably lead to happiness and prosperity. However, it all starts with a desire. It is impossible to visualize your existence without knowing what you want. Then, your purpose and life plan can coalesce around it. It is comparable to preparing cake batter without butter or eggs to bind the flour.

If you don't have a desire, you lack the motivation to plan your life because you lack the inspiration to do so! You respond, "What difference does it make?" "My existence is as it is." certainly, but if you are unhappy, you must make adjustments, and a desire always precedes change.

This is completely understandable, given that the undesirable things are constantly in your face: poor health, undesirable employment, a stressful relationship, and a lack of money.

These things are so disagreeable because they are so dissimilar to who you truly are! They are a persistent source of irritation, like fingernails scratching on a blackboard.

Nonetheless, it is also true that manifestation MUST commence with a clearly defined thought template.

This is how it functions in both the physical and non-physical realms. Actions are a precise reflection of thought in the physical world. Actions are effective and follow the path of least resistance when the mind is aligned with a positive and desirable purpose.

You control your life's direction because the universe responds to your vibrations. Your physical actions are significant but only an extension of your thoughts and intentions. Therefore, you must create a life plan.

When your energy is aligned with a profoundly felt personal desire, you will take action joyfully and without much effort, struggle, or strain. Note that we did not say "without effort."

Your action cycles may require tremendous effort but will be enjoyable labor. Have you ever begun an endeavor only to realize how much more work is required? When finished, you glance back and exclaim, "Wow! Did I do everything?"

Sometimes, you have yet to learn how you accomplished it! Along the way, you were joined by others who assisted, and the endeavor may have evolved unexpectedly. This occurs, however, when you connect with the creative energy of the universe. This energy is so potent that it can change the fate of your planet.

We want you to step into your authority and prevent "the elites from manipulating and controlling humanity. There is no manipulation because societies, governments, and economies always reflect the group's consciousness, and your existence will always reflect your beliefs perfectly.

If you want to change, start NOW to determine what you want! This is the most effective labor you will ever perform and requires neither a Congressional committee nor a Ph.D. nor per purpose from the authorities.

If sufficient numbers of people conducted this work, societies could be transformed in a startlingly short period. Institutions that no longer serve you would vanish, as they cannot survive on unsuitable vibrational terrain. This is the strength of intellect.

You are all highly effective co-creators. The universe has been designed to respond immediately to your thoughts and intentions.

This is the case because the physical universe and everything in it is a field of consciousness or subliminal energy that is extraordinarily and dynamically responsive to a change in your vibration.

Everything you perceive with your human senses is a vibrational interpretation of something so vast, majestic, and potent that you can't possibly comprehend it while you are still a human.

The Creative Principle's decisions and inventions created the universe through thought. The universe beyond the reach of human senses is so immense, and there are so many playable environments that it would astound you. We assert that EVERYTHING IS POSSIBLE!

Therefore, please start creating your desired existence RIGHT NOW! Don't procrastinate any longer! You can achieve anything you desire, but you must first trust you can, and it is much simpler to change your beliefs when you have the correct success formula -- one that functions with universal laws rather than against them!

CHAPTER 3: BENEFITS OF UNDERSTANDING YOUR PURPOSE.

Increasingly, people are searching for something more than just "making a living." They are becoming aware that something is absent from their lives and are experiencing an inner sense of discontent. Many outwardly successful individuals describe feeling "off-track" or feeling unfinished. That which is absent is a sense of purpose.

We need a purpose to drift aimlessly and unfulfilled through existence. According to business psychologist and psychotherapist Douglas La Bier, the consequences of not discovering one's purpose include chronic dissatisfaction, a lack of interior peace, and a sense of being out of sync with one's inner self.

Here are some benefits of identifying and pursuing your purpose:

1. It provides you control over your direction in life. You cease following the "shoulds" of family and society and set your course for what you want to do with your life.

2. You are more likely to have a positive life outlook and be stress-resistant.

3. You focus more on life, making decisions based on what is significant to you.

As you align yourself with what you were "made for," you experience greater inner serenity and fulfillment.

You live more in the natural flow of existence than in struggle. This isn't to say there aren't challenges, but when you have a sense of meaning and purpose, the challenges seem smaller, and you get through them more swiftly and easily. You are better able to manage life's ups and downs.

It redefines your concept of accomplishment. It's more than ascending the corporate ladder, having a specific title, or making much money. This isn't to say you can't make good money. When you do what you enjoy, you are more aligned with all your desires, including financial abundance.

The traditional indicators of success in our society are less significant than the inner gratification you derive from how you spend your time. Success is determined by what provides you happiness.

You will enjoy knowing that your efforts are contributing to a larger whole. When you are "on purpose," you will do what you love and utilize your skills to contribute more positive energy to the world. Serving beyond one's self-interest connects one to their higher nature. It opens the heart and calls forth the spirit.

You experience an increase in overall contentment and a greater zest for life!

Having a sense of purpose can increase your lifespan.

Congratulations if you've connected with your purpose! You are reaping the benefits of "doing what you love and believing it matters." Whatever you've discovered, if it is your passion and has significance to you, it does matter.

I encourage you to investigate the options if you need clarification on your purpose. What do you enjoy doing? Which abilities and skills do you appreciate employing? To go deeper, you can enlist a coach's assistance. The universe awaits your singular gifts!

CHAPTER 4: ARE YOU MOTIVATED BY YOUR LIFE'S PURPOSE?

I assure you that discovering your life's purpose is serious business! Therefore, you should take your life purpose seriously. Once is all you get, and you're not growing any younger. Everything comes to you in the ideal manner and timing.

I've been through enough turbulence in my life that anything that occurs now is 'Small Stuff,' and I can grin in the face of adversity. I am 100 percent confident that this is a transient annoyance.

Yes, a door opens for something greater to enter your life when things go awry. Never doubt that because it is so true; worrying about it only drags things down significantly.

You find yourself upset about something and give in to that emotion, clinging to it for all it's worth, which is nothing unless you consider the money a therapist could make off of you by treating your mental disorder. No one desires that!

Finding your life's purpose can be difficult but worth the effort. Don't let attempting to figure everything out at once drive you insane. It is a gradual process requiring patience and tender loving care. (not just for yourself but for the entire universe).

Occasionally, it is necessary to let go of all the serious matters in life and take the time to LAUGH! Observe a comedy or recall when you laughed so hard you could barely breathe.

If you can't find anything to laugh about, surround yourself with cheerful people or, even better, make someone else laugh. (do something stupid that works every time). It is infectious and gives you a great sensation as well.

Okay, if you can't make someone giggle, at least be kind to them (you CAN do that, right?). You already know the Law of Attraction, correct? What you give out, you will receive back. What travels around eventually returns. That is so accurate!

So, while your life's purpose drives you, please savor the journey. That is the whole point! It is about appreciating every instant you have been granted. Don't fret over the past and the future. Live in the present moment and make each day the greatest of your life!

Before you can start your search for your Life's Purpose, it would be beneficial to define "Purpose." Otherwise, you can search for something you may not even recognize if you discover it!

What Do We Specifically Mean by "Purpose"?

To determine one's purpose, it is helpful to comprehend one's context.

A context is characterized by: "The conditions under which an event takes place; a setting."

For example, a student's context, which is to study and earn high grades, defines their purpose. The responsibility of a police officer is to maintain Law and order in society. The purpose of a firefighter is to put out fires and assist the public. The purpose of a teacher is to educate and "teach" their students.

The issue with discovering one's purpose is related to one's current life role and self-awareness. If you identify yourself with your position as an employee, your purpose becomes the company's purpose. The same holds for self-identification as a parent, as your purpose is to nurture, nourish, educate, and best prepare your child for life.

The difficulty arises when your temporary function as an employee or parent changes and the purpose with which you have identified yourself ceases to exist. You abandon your "purpose" in life.

When you realize that many roles in human society are transitory, defining your life's purpose must be something that can withstand the test of time.

The Setting of Life.

Observe nature for a clue to help you define your life's purpose. Why observe nature? The notion of having a life purpose implies that you are on earth for a specific reason, and if you're here to do something, it must likely be related to achieving a worthwhile purpose in the context of the bigger picture.

Taking a cue from nature, it is evident that life is perpetually evolving and expanding. Nature doesn't cease. It simply grows and changes over time to acclimate to varying environmental conditions.

The question is how to relate an abstract concept such as growth and development to everyday existence.

In this case, the concept of having two levels of Life Purpose may be useful:

1. The Ultimate Life Purpose.

2. The Self-Selected Life Purpose.

The Greater Life Purpose.

Higher levels of your life purpose are referred to by the term Higher Life Purpose. This refers to the portions of your existence and Purpose that would be permanent and consistent throughout your existence.

For instance, the first element of continuous growth, development, and evolution may continue to be a component of your life's purpose. Depending on your Self-Chosen Purpose, you would continue to develop and evolve in a specific manner. Regardless of where you are, continuous growth and development will continue to assist you in your personal development.

The second aspect of the Higher Life Purpose may incorporate the concept of creating value and benefit for oneself and others. Since we don't exist in isolation from other people, whatever you choose to do must be of some benefit not only to yourself but also to others.

This makes sense, given that if you did something that benefited you at the expense of others, sooner or later, you would receive negative feedback that would reduce the benefits you derived from your actions, either in direct action from others or emotional dissonance from within.

The third component of a Higher Life Purpose could involve maximizing your potential. By potential, I mean your latent abilities, strengths, talents, and other distinctive or available characteristics.

You could utilize your abilities in any profession or endeavor. Being athletically gifted could enable you to participate in different sports, including tennis, golf, and football. Possessing athletic ability is a talent that would enable you to participate in virtually any sport. The only remaining issue is which sport you would excel in. Your Self-Selected Life Purpose would then determine the manifestation of your Higher Life Purpose.

CHAPTER 5: THE KEY TO PURPOSE.

Since it requires effort and self-control, most individuals never live a life of meaning. Most individuals accept whatever comes their way. They exist in a state of silent destitution. They discuss what they should do and have grand aspirations but have yet to take action. A life devoid of action is a life devoid of purpose.

Success has been researched and examined for many years. We have more information on success than ever before, and one striking similarity among life's champions is that they all have a clear purpose. It is your purpose that propels you forward.

Your purpose gives you impetus. We must be aware of our development and contributions. Each time you achieve a purpose, your self-esteem will increase, and you'll build on that success like an avalanche gaining momentum as it moves forward. Therefore, winners have purposes and a significant life purpose.

Human beings are not lazy. They merely have ineffectual purposes, i.e., purposes that don't motivate them. Some individuals wake up intending to go to work. Go back home, recline in front of the television, consume a few brews, and retire to bed, only to repeat the same routine the following day, the day after, and the day after.

If you lack a significant purpose in life, you will forever be subject to the authority of those who do.

Many individuals in hospitals, prisons, and the legal system lack a significant purpose. Without a purpose, there is no compelling future to anticipate. Without a compelling future, you give up on life and fall into an unproductive mental state, and as a result of the Law of attraction, you attract more melancholy and more of the things you don't want.

Without a compelling future, people resort to drugs and alcohol to change their state of mind; however, this is only a temporary solution, which is why it is repeatedly used.

If you don't grow in this existence, you will perish. This world will destroy you just as nature destroys vegetation and animals. Consider all the objects in your world that once served a function you no longer require. These items have been discarded because they are no longer useful to you.

It's okay if you don't know your life's overarching purpose. Most individuals need to be made aware of their purpose. According to estimates, only about three percent of the population has clear life purposes. Your purpose will emerge as you learn to set small goals aligning with your values. Some individuals determine their purpose young, while others wait until much later.

In his sixties, Colonel Sanders founded Kentucky Fried Chicken, or KFC, as it is known today. He stated, "At that time, I resolved to accomplish something worthwhile if I could, and no amount of hours, labor, or money would prevent me from giving my best."

Here are twelve principles and action patterns that have worked for me and many others, which you can use to discover your major purpose or purpose.

Some individuals don't set purposes because they believe they don't merit them. They have low self-esteem and self-worth. They lack self-confidence and believe no one else does either.

If you have low self-esteem, I can tell you until the end that you must believe in yourself, but it won't matter. You can only increase your self-esteem by starting with small purposes and gaining momentum.

1. Start by constructively serving others. This will also improve your self-esteem. Volunteer at a local church, civic organization, or hospital to start. Einstein was once asked why we are here. He paused and stated that our purpose is to serve others.

2. Pursue your passion, not your profits. Some individuals need a defined purpose because they believe it would not be financially rewarding. I have discovered that money makes no difference if you do what you enjoy. The funds will arrive. If you enjoy your work, you will labor hard and not mind. You enjoy it so much that you would do it for free if you weren't paid.

3. Determine what you value. When you start to establish purposes, they must align with your values. Create an enumeration of your values and assign each one a number from one to ten.

First, being the most essential value, and so on. If your relationships are your top priority, place them first. If you place the highest value on your well-being, put a number one there. Only you are aware of your utmost worth.

4. Surround yourself with successful, optimistic individuals. You'd be astonished at how eager successful people are to assist you with answers if you're willing to ask questions. "Better to be rebuked

by a wise man than praised by a fool," said King Solomon.

As you start working on this area, it is okay to abandon old, negative friendships. Don't be surprised if your former friends consider you unsuccessful. Some so-called acquaintances don't wish you well because they want you to be as unhappy as they are. Don't let them hinder your progress.

5. Write down your purposes. Most people never write down their purposes because they believe they already know what they are and therefore have no need to do so. Winners in life record their purposes with clarity and concentration.

Simply by writing down your purposes, the Law of attraction works for you. You will start to attract the things on which you concentrate the most. It would be best to have a single, overarching purpose or purpose, followed by a series of sub-purposes to support it.

When I began earning my black belt in Kenpo karate, I knew that the black belt was the ultimate purpose but that the first belt was the most essential. The lesser purposes will always support the larger purposes. Write your purposes in the present tense, as if they already existed.

6. Document your purposes with a deadline. Set a deadline for yourself to complete each purpose. Ensure that each purpose is measurable. For instance, you can measure a salary increase or weight loss.

7. Determine the price you will be required to pay. I'm aware of what you're saying. Purchase it? Yes, this is what I mean.

What will you need to learn to achieve your purpose?

How long must you work to obtain it?

Are you willing to remain up late and rise early to complete it?

Are you willing to exert yourself?

If you can't answer these queries, you lack a commitment to your purpose. It would be best if you bore the cost. There are no complimentary meals in this world. You must pay in advance.

8. Write down every reason you can think of to support your primary purpose or purpose. Why are you laboring toward this purpose? According to research, if we have reasons for our purposes, we are more likely to maintain focus on the purpose at hand.

I do what I do because individuals told me I couldn't accomplish what I said I wanted. They would either guffaw or roll their eyes and leave. Some were also members of my family. Consider reasons that will motivate you. Reasons that will re-energize you when you need it most.

9. Create a plan and implement it. Write out your plan in detail. Approximately every three months, reevaluate your position. With a plan, you can construct something that will last. Consider where you wish to go and where you are now.

Built from the ground up, just like an enormous skyscraper, the foundation's depth determines a structure's height. Develop a solid foundation by preparing for action with a solid plan.

Ensure that your primary purpose serves people in a virtuous manner. When you do so, you will acquire your respect and the respect of those around you. Be gracious, patient, and kind to others.

Consider the principle of sowing and reaping. You will reap an excellent harvest every time you sow good seed. The greatest present you can ever give is yourself. Kindness, patience, and generosity contribute to developing one's character and inner fortitude.

10. Be daring. We enter this world fearless of new adventures and unconcerned with what others may say or think. The human intellect is designed for greatness, but we become programmed for failure as we mature. Both the fear of falling and the fear of loud noises are innate. All other concerns are acquired as

we age. Fears are learned and conditioned responses, which is a plus.

This indicates that we can unlearn and recondition our behaviors. The most effective method for overcoming fear is action. Make daily action a habit. The action routine will increase your confidence and self-esteem.

11. Take the initiative. As soon as you've completed the preceding steps, take action toward your purposes. Action will assist in gaining momentum. Isaac Newton taught us that an object will be in motion once an object is set until an external force acts upon it. Hence, take action now. Now, if some external factor appears to send you off course, which it will, you will be thrown off.

Gather other data, reevaluate your options, and, if necessary, change your strategy. When a plane departs from Dallas with a destination of New York, it is often off course. The pilot makes constant adjustments to maintain the aircraft on course.

The pilot is aware of the destination and maintains flight in that direction. The same holds when pursuing your main life purposes. You will occasionally veer off course, but if you have the self-discipline to change your course and maintain forward momentum, you will reach your destination.

12. Daily review of your purposes list. We know our minds can only contain one dominant thought at a time. According to the Bible, "As a man thinks, so is he."

When you review your purposes daily, you initiate the attraction process. You will start to observe things that will bring you closer to your purpose. People will arrive to assist. You will discover resources that previously existed. The universe will support you. The objects you seek are also searching for you.

Now, will it be difficult? Yes! Will there be moments when you feel like giving up? Yes!

Will there be instances when people will abandon you and disappoint you? Yes!

Will everything transpire overnight for you? No!

However, if you follow these steps, remain persistent, and continue to learn and grow from successful people, you will reach your purpose much more quickly.

It is not what you say, plan, intend, or aspire for that ultimately matters; it is what you do. A life devoid of action is a life devoid of purpose. Live your existence with intention. Ask yourself: why am I here?

CHAPTER 6: HOW TO DISCOVER YOUR LIFE'S PURPOSE IMMEDIATELY.

The fulfillment of one's life purpose brings immeasurable joy, which in turn promotes robust health and physical well-being.

Does your life's meaning appear to elude you? Are you uncertain of your "Life Purpose"? You have just discovered it!

You can be thinking to yourself, "Yeah, right!" How could this be? "All this time, I've been searching for my life's purpose, and now this nut says I've found it!" - Acceptable enough. Let me clarify.

We need to be more precise with the purpose of our lives. We believe that if something is not mysterious and extraordinary, it can't be it. However, I would like to inquire. What do you believe your life's purpose of being?

If we "zero base" it, which means to make it as straightforward as possible, you are happiest when you are in harmony with the universe's natural laws. (pure physics, mind you). The Law of service, one of the natural laws, illustrates the point well. Spiritual development is the ultimate purpose of our lives (even if we don't initially recognize it).

The way we conduct ourselves daily is also straightforward. To sustain the experience, we must maintain our own lives. For this to occur, we must labor to provide for ourselves, and being on purpose entails being happy while adding value and solving the "urgent problems" of others.

Whether you clean homes for a living or manage multi-national corporations, you are living on purpose when you are excited to start each day because it represents another chance to add value to the lives of others.

You can see that the creator of all life has encoded a very simple program in each of us: "Become better than you are while helping your neighbor do the same!" Within our daily activities, we discover the opportunity and the lessons required to implement this program.

The purpose of this existence is to learn as much as possible, and these opportunities enable us to make the necessary attitude choices to maximize our educational potential.

You believe our purpose as spiritual beings to have a physical experience is to grow and approach perfection. In doing so, we assist those around us in doing the same, enhancing collective consciousness. Making the universe a better place for everyone starts with a single individual.

Precessional effect.

Buckminster Fuller explained it best. The occurrence of 'Precession,' distinct from 'Procession,' is an inevitable consequence of our actions. Professional activity is founded on linear action and whose outcome results from a deliberate plan.

A precessional effect is a side-effect often unexpected and typically operates at right angles to the 'Processional' effects.

In nature, precessional secondary effects are readily apparent. Bees are an excellent example. The bee needs honey, so it flies from flower to flower accumulating nectar due to a deliberate and direct chain of causes and effects. However, due to this activity's precessional side effect, flowers are pollinated, resulting in different attractive and necessary natural effects.

In His wisdom, the Great Spirit gave bees and humans the need to work to provide for self,' knowing that precession would take care of the rest, thereby ensuring the daily fulfillment of his creatures' purposes.

The greater your awareness of yourself and the need to add value to the lives of others, the greater the value of your precessional impact. Also, this is how we can change the world together, one person at a time.

Reason and Effect.

The precessional aspect of our activity is the consequence of our actions. When searching for your life's purpose, you only need to respond yes to three simple questions.

Am I adding value and having a significant positive impact on the lives of each and every persons I encounter?

Am I genuinely speaking from the heart, and do I have the best interests of others in mind (and not just my own)?

Am I genuinely content with this pursuit?

Does it fill my spirit with joy?

Your precessional effect on this world doesn't require outward material success and recognition, though you can undoubtedly desire and (ultimately) receive it. What it does require, however, is that you diligently pursue your heart's desires.

Whether or not you answered "yes" to the questions above, you are fundamentally living out your life's purpose. However, the optimal scenario is for you to be able to answer YES and fulfill that purpose with enthusiasm.

However, be realistic about it; even if you answered yes to the questions above, you would still be satisfied with your activity 100 percent of the time. The key is to respect yourself and start making changes (first within yourself) to facilitate a change in your external circumstances.

How do I change my course?

Here are a few suggestions to help you start fulfilling your life purpose with joy:

Get crystal clarity.

First, you must assess your current situation and desired destination. Clarify the straightforward aspects of your daily activities that bring you joy and benefit others and start doing this more often, whenever feasible. Keeping a journal and putting down your thoughts, meditation, emotional freedom techniques, and even prayer are all processes that can assist you in gaining clarity.

Concentrate on your virtues.

Using your assets to add value to yourself and others is the one thing that will make you the happiest and most successful. Any professional athlete will tell you that they focus on bringing their weaknesses up to a competent level, but with the utmost concentration and zeal, they strive to improve their strengths!

Consider your emotions.

If you dislike doing something, cease doing it. Get an education, develop your creativity, and do what you enjoy. Life is too brief to be unhappy. Take RESPONSIBILITY for your actions, be wise about your shift in focus, and remember the words of the great motivational speaker Zig Ziglar: "You can have everything you want in life as long as you help enough other people get what they want!"

Face your fears.

Ralph Waldo Emerson stated, "Nature is not capricious, and the implantation of a desire indicates that its fulfillment is inherent in the creature that feels it." Simply put, you would not have a desire if you could not achieve it. Have confidence in yourself and overcome your anxieties.

Persist.

Your commitment will be consistently and seemingly aggressively challenged throughout your lifetime. Prepare for this. Just because you are "on purpose" doesn't imply that everything will always be easy; we have much to learn! Too many states they 'want' and 'will,' but too few actually 'get' and 'do' - not because they can't but because they RESIST - often just as they are about to achieve the desired outcome.

Don't allow this to occur; have confidence in yourself. Replace negative beliefs with a new mantra: "Regardless of how bad or difficult it gets, I WILL MAKE IT!"

CHAPTER 7: HOW TO CONNECT WITH YOUR LIFE'S PURPOSE.

"What is the meaning of my life?" Does this ring a bell?

Almost everyone has undoubtedly wondered this at some point. Occasionally, a simple, fleeting question will enter one's consciousness. However, it can sometimes feel like a heartbreaking, too-daunting endeavor.

The answers to the age-old queries regarding your life's purpose can be found in the knowledge that has been with us for centuries. Each of us has a unique life purpose; it is up to you to discover your unique aptitude, which will help you determine your life purpose.

"However, how do I discover my life's purpose?"

The principle of the Law of purpose provides the answer to this inquiry. This universal principle pertains to all individuals at all times and locations and has done so throughout history.

Many names know the Law of Purpose, and its powerful universal existence asserts that each of us can discover our life's purpose and that, once discovered, we can use this priceless knowledge to attain ultimate and enduring happiness, even bliss. You can discover your life's purpose by following what this Law instructs us.

The initial step in learning how to use the Law of purpose to discover your life's purpose is to decide to do so. This is simple, but it can also be extremely complicated. The difficulty is that the Law of Attraction states that our thoughts and words will manifest as reality.

Guess what happens if an individual consistently claims to have no life purpose? They're correct—each time. To use the Law of Attraction to discover your life's purpose, you must first determine that.

"My life has a purpose."

Once you have decided, you can determine your life's purpose. Step two is to discover and express your unique aptitude. Each of us has a special talent for something.

Consider the activities you appreciate doing the most and appear to excel at. You've already decided in the first stage, so it's too late to say you don't have one. Remember that due to the Law of Attraction, you are always correct.

Consider yourself and your unique skills with care. Once you recognize this talent, cultivate it, apply it, and immerse yourself in its expression. When you do so, the benefits of enjoying your work will manifest. You will feel closer to your purpose of discovering your life purpose and experiencing the happiness that comes with it.

"How do I know I've discovered my life's purpose?"

Once you utilize your abilities and share them with others, many opportunities will present themselves. You will experience your life and your life's purpose and feel at ease with yourself.

Instead of worrying about why you don't know your life's purpose, you will recognize the things in life that help you evolve and appreciate the world around you. Follow the Law of Attraction; the more you appreciate your distinctive qualities, the clearer your life's purpose will become.

CHAPTER 8: MISCONCEPTIONS ABOUT LIFE PURPOSE.

Many things need to be clarified about the meaning of existence. These misunderstandings cause many individuals to unnecessarily tangle themselves in chains while attempting to determine why they are here.

I will dispel the following common misconceptions about function.

Not everyone has a purpose in life. We are all born for a specific reason. The heart is the source of one's purpose. It is what you enjoy doing. There is a reason for your presence here. The fact that you are reading this and contemplating your life's purpose indicates that you have one!

Some purposes are greater and more noble than others. They have a greater impact.

Comparison is never prudent. We are all unique individuals who entered this world with our desires, talents, interests, and purposes. Your purpose is yours. Being a major influencer or establishing significant foundations to achieve your purposes is unnecessary. This is the path for some individuals, but for the vast majority, it is not.

And you can't accurately assess your impact!

For instance, I loved being a lower elementary Montessori teacher but didn't know how profoundly I had impacted some of my students at the time.

After leaving the classroom, I began to hear from former students as young adults. They told me that their experience in my class had instilled a lifelong passion for learning and prepared them well for everything that followed their graduation. Their Montessori years were remembered with affection and admiration. I realized that the improvement of even a few lives was significant.

Your life's purpose will necessitate effort and sacrifice.

The opposite is true. When you're doing what you adore, you infuse it with love, and I'll say it again: your purpose is always to do what you adore. It utilizes both your innate and acquired abilities. Even if there are difficulties, you'll be so pleased with what you're doing that you won't consider them difficult.

As we progress through life, we evolve and develop. Our purpose may also evolve. It may not be entirely different, but how you express it may change. I was intentional as a teacher, and I am intentional as a coach.

It is possible to have multiple purposes. For instance, you could have a purpose in rearing your children to be the best versions of themselves and pursue a fulfilling career.

Everyone's purpose is to expand into more compassion. The activities we engage in daily contribute to this end. What we do is less important than who we become in the process.

If others are doing it, it is not my intention.

With 7 billion individuals, someone must be doing the same thing as you. This is a good occurrence.

Yes, you are distinct! And you will perform that activity in a manner distinct from that of others.

You will discover that you resonate with the people (or animals or plants) you are intended to serve.

We all want to discover our life's work because we want to do meaningful, fulfilling labor. Everyone deserves that! Your purpose can undoubtedly involve your career.

But purpose also extends beyond your career. It pertains to your spiritual development. This can be achieved through your life's work or other experiences, such as parenthood, volunteering, caring for a sick loved one, and being a good friend.

I can't make a livelihood doing what I enjoy.

This is a widespread concern. Consider how many individuals are earning a living doing what they enjoy. There are many instances. When you are enthusiastic about your profession, you will achieve success. You won't allow anything to stand in your way.

It is also prudent to consider how you define a comfortable lifestyle. You are in abundance if you have everything you need when you need it. I'm not suggesting just slipping by. You are unquestionably wealthy if you can live a healthy lifestyle and have a comfortable home, savings, and enjoyable opportunities.

Therefore, focus on what you enjoy and what you excel at. Avoid self-censorship in any way possible. Consider with gratitude the obstacles you've overcome in your existence. In the end, your stated purpose is accurate.

CHAPTER 9: REASONS WHY INDIVIDUALS DON'T LIVE THEIR PASSIONS.

Many individuals claim they don't have the opportunity to pursue life changes. However appealing, going in a different direction appears too daunting. There needs to be more commitment to doing what is necessary to move into a more fulfilling existence because the task appears too daunting.

They fret about obligations to other things that are indeed essential, such as family and their current source of income. Then, movement ceases, and existence continues in the same unsatisfactory pattern.

The first thing to realize if you feel like there is no time to make the changes necessary to live a life aligned with your passions and purpose is that you don't need to do everything at once. Here, take a breath! This is a slow-moving procedure. There's no hurry. Create a simple list of the steps you believe will be required to achieve your purpose.

Consider the various domains or categories involved in achieving your purpose. Then, list the necessary measures to accomplish them. Devote 30 minutes to completing this initial step. That is all—just 30 minutes.

Then, you can prioritize the action steps that you've developed. What can you do today to advance closer to your purpose? You can select one action step per day or week. It makes no difference so long as you are consistent. One step at a time is significantly more manageable than considering the entire process. Some processes will require very little time. Check them off as you complete them and celebrate your success.

Your brain enjoys the sensation of development! Waiting until significant purposes are achieved is too long before celebrating. Your celebration can be as simple as pumping your forearm or congratulating yourself. Acknowledge your achievement.

Before taking action, ensure you have completed the "emotional journey." Any action you take out of a sense of obligation, i.e., when you don't feel good about it, will not be successful. It will be effective when an actor feels like the logical next step, and you feel alive or excited about it.

Some steps will challenge your comfort zone, which is acceptable. We must leave our comfort zones to develop and expand. It requires practice distinguishing between a red flag indicating "Don't go there now" and the sensation of stepping outside your comfort zone. The major way to figure it out is to perform the action and observe the results. You can always correct your course if you take the incorrect action.

An obligation is a judgment. Determine how you will lead your existence. Do you wish to conclude your life without having accomplished the things you felt in your heart you were destined to do? What would that be like? Today, commit to yourself and the world you were intended to serve and take that first step!

Conscious and unconscious beliefs are one of the greatest obstacles people confront when attempting to live by following their passions and purpose. Our beliefs dictate what we attract and allow to enter our lives. When we start with limiting or erroneous premises, it hinders our ability to achieve our purposes and desires.

Examples of common limiting beliefs include:

"I am too old to initiate a new endeavor."

"Only a handful of exceptionally talented individuals achieve their purposes."

It is simply a matter of fate.

"I'm simply not good enough (talented, skilled, educated)."

Nobody will be interested in what I have to offer.

"I don't matter."

Nobody can flourish in the current economy.

"I don't deserve to receive what I desire."

Errors and failure are undesirable.

The inventory is extensive! It is essential to realize that your beliefs create your reality. Your beliefs, which are often unconscious, result from years of "programming" by your parents, teachers, religious leaders, and personal observations of the reactions of others and society.

They were most likely downloaded into you before the age of six when your brain was operating in delta and theta waves, which correspond to sleep or trance in an adult. In other terms, the brain is extremely vulnerable during this time. These individuals may have been well-intentioned, but all operated according to their programming.

According to neuroscientists, up to 95% of our consciousness is subliminal. Our values, attitudes, and convictions are stored in the subconscious mind. Suppose you have been unsuccessful in achieving a purpose despite doing everything "right" and possibly employing the principles of the Law of attraction. In that case, the problem likely originates from your subconscious beliefs.

You can even comprehend consciously that you deserve what you desire or that it's okay to make mistakes, but if your subconscious disagrees, your efforts will fail. Our beliefs determine how we perceive the world. Through this lens, everything we see and experience is filtered.

For instance, if you believe that the only way to achieve success is through hard labor and struggle, then that is the only way you will achieve success. People do it, but it's miserable! If you believe you are too old or unimportant, you will only get started if you recognize and change this belief.

Consider your current state of affairs if you want to determine your beliefs. The good, the evil, and the ugly have all been produced by your belief system. Consider what a person must have believed to have created this.

One way to consider a belief is that it is merely a recurring thought. Challenge your limiting assumptions! Happy individuals don't believe everything they believe. Old beliefs can be changed and supplanted with beliefs that better serve your current self.

Start by telling yourself that you can and will achieve your purposes. Replace every time you think of reasons why you can't do what you want with reasons why you can. Create a list of all the reasons you can accomplish your purposes.

Neuroplasticity is a property discovered by scientists in the brain. In other terms, an old dog can be taught new tricks! By focusing on the new concepts, we can create new neural pathways and eliminate old, ineffective ones.

Consider it as creating a new path through the undergrowth. The ancient path is overgrown due to lack of use. This requires concentration and perseverance, but it is worthwhile.

EFT or meridian tapping, PSYCH-K®, and hypnotherapy are a few techniques that can speed up the healing process. All these allow easy access to the subconscious and shift the brain into a receptive state, allowing old, limiting beliefs to be supplanted with new, empowering ones. The world awaits your talents, and you have a right to live a life you enjoy.

CHAPTER 10: EMBARKING ON YOUR LIFE'S PURPOSE JOURNEY.

The purpose is more than a path; it is a journey that starts with birth and ends with death. There is so much to see and experience on this voyage that it requires a lifetime. But there is a direction to purpose, and it requires considerable navigation. It is more important to point in the correct direction than to reach a specific destination.

In today's society, it is all about the destination, and we strive to reach it so quickly that we cross the finish line in the flash of an eye without ever running the race. This way of reasoning only leads to discontentment.

How can you appreciate crossing the finish line if you have yet to endure the obstacles and difficulties of the race?

It is as if you were attempting to enjoy the sensation of drinking a cold glass of water when you are extremely thirsty, but you are not thirsty at all. It will never truly satiate you if you have not developed a genuine desire for it.

Today, more and more individuals recognize the importance of voyage enjoyment, increasing numbers of self-help and personal development. The authors discuss savoring the present, living in the moment, and being fully present.

All you have right now is indeed the present moment. In an instant, it will be gone forever, and you will never be able to recover it. The future is nothing but a fantasy. You comprehend this from a philosophical standpoint. But if you are experiencing tension, anxiety, and frustration, you are not following this universal Law: live in the Present.

It seems simple to say, "Okay, I'll just enjoy the moment." Then, within minutes of making that statement, a thought will come to mind about how you're supposed to be doing this and remember that you promised so-and-so you'd do that, and there are provisions for dinner tonight, and what about the children? Are you today's carpool driver?

If it's not an evil notion from your ego attempting to perpetuate a state of internal stress, it's a circumstance or person attempting to pull you into their drama. When you declare your intention to live in the present, life will send you to curve balls quicker than a speeding bullet.

Your purpose is to live in the present moment and experience all the roadblocks, highs, and lows. Just as you question, "Why am I here?" Remember that the answer is to discover it daily, here and now.

Today, you are meant to be where you are on your path to happiness. How are you feeling today? Then, decide in the present which direction you want to point to tomorrow. That is your purpose, to continually choose your course of action.

Having a Self-Selected Life Purpose would allow expressing your Higher Life Purpose. The many aspects of Higher Life Purpose could be more specific for daily application.

It makes sense to be able to choose how your Higher Life Purpose is expressed, particularly if you believe in "free will."

Your Self-Selected Life Purpose is then a combination of your characteristics and involvement in something beneficial to society.

This is where a solid understanding of oneself is beneficial. When you can find a good match between your characteristics and a vocation and your desire and passion for the work, you have a very good outlet for expressing your Life Purpose.

If you have a musical aptitude, you can find satisfaction in expressing yourself through singing, composing, playing an instrument, or other means. If your aptitude lies in teaching and education, you can decide that you would like to pursue a career in teaching. If your skill lies in maintaining order and discipline, consider a career as a law enforcement officer.

There is no "correct" or "incorrect" response. You will ultimately experience fulfillment and happiness when aligned with your selected purpose.

By dividing your Life Purpose into two categories, you have created something fundamentally permanent and adaptable to varying life circumstances. Your Higher Life Purpose would remain relatively constant, whereas your Self-Chosen Life Purpose would permit you to adapt and express yourself in response to environmental changes.

CHAPTER 11: DO YOU FEEL THAT YOUR EXISTENCE IS LACKING SOMETHING?

We are all born for a specific reason. We are unique and have a special function that no one else can perform. When we discover, recognize, and act upon that, we experience fulfillment. When we don't, we feel as though we are just going through the motions of existence, and therein lies the feeling that something is lacking.

To their credit, people everywhere realize they want their career to be about more than just money. They desire to fulfill the purpose for which they were created. They want their work to be engaging, enjoyable, and aligned with their passions.

They desire that their distinctive abilities and skills be utilized. When this occurs, you are living purposefully and will be replete with happiness, vitality, and abundance.

Significant Work.

We require our labor to have significance. When we engage in work that we enjoy, we increase the abundance in our lives. When we compel ourselves to engage in activities that are not meaningful to us, we disrupt the flow.

This will often manifest in your finances and health. Decide now that you deserve to do what you adore and the people (or animals or environment) you are meant to serve.

Your work can evolve as you develop over time. What once represented your purpose may no longer do so now. Each time you transition, you will utilize your talents and skills in a novel way.

My purpose, for instance, is to motivate others to be the finest version of themselves and to live joyfully. You need not necessarily change jobs to fulfill your purpose. No matter where you are, you can affect people with your open heart and spread positive emotions. Determine what you can do so that you can add more light and a higher vibration to your workplace if you already enjoy your work.

Can purpose be communicated through activities other than our means of subsistence?

It is unnecessary to be employed or in commerce to contribute. You can fulfill your purpose through interests or community-based activities. You can discover your purpose by guiding your children to be their best selves or caring for an elderly or ailing relative who requires assistance and a loving spirit to uplift them.

Your purpose may consist of embodying and propagating the vibration of joy wherever you go. This could include any employment or none at all.

How do your spiritual development and your unique contribution intersect?

You develop as you focus on how life guides you to discover and act on your purpose. You live with increased presence, awareness, and cognizance.

"Achieving enlightenment requires learning to incorporate awareness and consciousness into everything you do, bringing the surrounding energy into greater harmony, beauty, and order. Your life's work is a vehicle for enlightenment and spiritual development because when you enjoy what you do, you naturally apply mindfulness to all your activities.

Then, how does your existence lead you to your purpose?

What circumstances or significant life events have led you down a particular path?

What do you enjoy doing?

You'll know you've found it based on how wonderful you feel!

CHAPTER 12: HOW TO EXPRESS YOUR LIFE'S PURPOSE THROUGH SELF-WORTH.

The belief that what they have to offer the world is of no value is one of the most pervasive emotions that prevent individuals from embracing their highest calling, their Divine Purpose. We are our own harshest critics, and when we consider the accomplishments of those who came before us, we ponder how we could do or say it differently.

Who am I to be doing this?

Who would care about what I have to say?

Or "Why would anyone use my services?" come to mind when we consider placing ourselves there.

People hold themselves back out of fear that they are not good enough; that their contributions are unimportant.

You are Not Alone.

I am quite acquainted with these emotions. When I first began to acquire clarity and sense the pull toward my purpose, this was what I thought. Thankfully, my desire to do what I desired eventually overcame my fears, and I began to pose alternative questions, such as, "What do I need to do to be of service?" "How can I put myself in a position to accomplish my purposes?"

I received the answers that would compel me to live my passions and achieve my purpose as soon as I began to ask the appropriate questions. I took action based on these answers, guided at every stage by what felt good and right to me.

When we limit ourselves out of fear of insufficiency, we deprive those awaiting our gifts of what THEY require. Fearing to pursue our passions and live lives that elevate and feel meaningful to us is selfish.

The focus is on one's concerns rather than the assistance one can provide to others. People are currently eager for what you have to offer. The greatest act of love we can perform for the world is to love and believe in ourselves to the extent that we are willing to be our finest.

Without exception, we all have a divine purpose. This doesn't imply that you must be prominent or establish foundations. You are simply getting in touch with what you most enjoy doing and taking the necessary steps to pursue it.

When faced with a decision or a choice, always choose in favor of your passions. You can offer your gifts to those waiting to receive them, whether people, animals, plants, or the earth itself if you follow your highest pleasure with fortitude.

You Have Value.

Without exception, we are all valuable. There is nothing you must demonstrate or accomplish to acquire your value. Simply by existing, you possess value. You are a part of All-That-Is and possess more power, wisdom, and love than you could ever fathom.

It is quite natural for moments of self-doubt to emerge intermittently as we travel through this physical voyage. We have, after all, been practicing emotions of insufficiency for most of our lives. Therefore, the solution is to form a new habit: the habit of affirming ourselves.

Here is a method you can employ:

Find a peaceful spot where you won't be interrupted and a comfortable position to recline. Take many slow, steady breaths and concentrate on relaxing your body. Send compassion and relaxation to any areas of tension that you can be aware of. Imagine breathing into your heart as you position one hand over your heart.

As you exhale, release any negative sentiments of fear. Inhale while contemplating "infinite love, " "inner peace," or whatever feels nice. Continue to discharge any unwanted emotions with each exhale. Imagine the negative thoughts departing your body as a gray mist. Continue for as long as you desire or until you experience a profound sense of serenity, ease, and flow.

While maintaining your hand over your heart, affirm, "I am a valuable individual. My purpose is significant. The things I create are even greater than I could have imagined, and I am supported as I pursue my highest calling."

Imagine that you are already living following your passions and your purpose. Immerse yourself in the emotions you anticipate and visualize yourself interacting with the people or other entities who will benefit from your gifts.

Feel gratitude for this amazing existence and your joy for following your heart. Use all your senses to make this mental image as vivid as possible. What do you hear, see, smell and taste? Enjoy yourself and have fun with this. It can be at most 5 minutes per day. Practice consistency is the key.

By recognizing your value, believing in your contribution's worth, and taking inspired action, you will enrich yourself and everyone you encounter.

CHAPTER 13: WHO ARE YOU, AND WHAT ARE YOU LOOKING FOR?

What is the point of living? I always say that happiness is the purpose of existence. I truly believe this. The purpose of your existence is to appreciate each day. It is also your responsibility to discover your purpose and enrich your existence.

Consider how you spend your time, the type of work you do, the nature of your family life, the type of people you are drawn to, and your interests.

What are you expressing throughout your life?

Are you leading the existence you desire? If not, then why?

Perhaps you are simply experiencing your "reality" and finding countless excuses not to pursue your dreams. Excuses are the number one reason for your lack of happiness and success. Excuses contribute to negativity, procrastination, tension, and depression. 'Reality 'Only exists once it is accepted in mind. You can create your reality regardless of the circumstances.

Everyone was created for a specific reason. Discovering your life's purpose allows you to connect with your source and assist others. Your purpose is determined more by WHO you are than WHAT you do.

Your life's purpose includes your values, identity, and deepest desires. When you live your life purposefully, you know your reason for being in the world. Examine your existence and determine your priorities.

Discovering your purpose is simple when you know who you are and what you truly desire. If you are dissatisfied with your circumstances, you must make adjustments. Select a purpose or purpose that will improve your existence.

The following questions will help you discover your life's purpose. You must WRITE down all your answers on paper.

Define three to five of your most significant values. Your values are the beliefs that matter most to you and guide your daily decisions. You are aligned and content when your actions and behavior align with your values. For instance, my values include Joy, Authenticity, Honesty, Spirituality, and Bravery.

How do you envision your optimal lifestyle?

Imagine having unlimited funds to do whatever you please.

What changes would you recommend?

Describe your ideal existence in the following areas:

Family, relationships, professional, health, finances, and spirituality.

How do you wish to utilize your time?

How would you spend your time differently if you only had three months to live?

Describe each hour of the day, including your desired wake-up time, work hours, family time, and time for yourself. Remember that this is your ideal existence. Refrain from thinking about money or circumstances preventing you from achieving your purpose. Consider YOUR reality, the one you can and wish to create.

What have you always desired to become? Write down your dream employment, whether a famous author, someone who travels the world helping people, or a race car driver.

What provides you with the most pleasure and satisfaction? Write down what truly brings you joy: people, events, activities, initiatives, and hobbies. Consider the matter carefully.

What talent or trait would you like to possess?

What are your interests?

What can you do for 24 hours and want to continue doing?

Choose one skill that you would like to master and develop.

What do you wish to be your legacy?

What are your contributions to society?

Consider whether you make a difference in the lives of others.

Remember not to consider money or justifications when answering these queries. The money follows when you discover your purpose and DO what you adore. A personal purpose has three components:

What do you enjoy doing?

Whom do you wish to assist?

What is the outcome or value you will create?

My life's purpose is to be happy daily, live with authenticity and faith, and assist others in discovering their happiness by concentrating on their words, thoughts, feelings, and emotions. Together, we can improve the world, one life at a time!

Commence living your purpose immediately. Clarify who you are and what you want and act accordingly to achieve contentment in your life. Fill your life with love, and have faith in your ability to create the life you deserve while helping others.

Periodically reevaluate your "life purpose" and modify it to reflect your current circumstances. Your purpose will need to be consistent despite the cyclical nature of life.

CHAPTER 14: VISION BOARDS FOR YOUR LIFE'S PURPOSE.

The science behind the Law of purpose is based on knowing how to manifest in a manner that eases any vibrational resistance so that you can manifest everything important to you as you fulfill your Life Purpose with clarity, purpose, life/work balance, and more vibrancy and prosperity.

This may include the creation of a vision board designed to attract more clients who resonate with your message, story, vision, or purpose and your desire to rehabilitate or assist others in enhancing their health and well-being.

What is a Life Purpose Vision Board?

It resembles a traditional vision board in that it visually represents your purposes. But I named my vision board the Life Purpose Vision Board to align my life purpose with the essence of who I am and to live a balanced existence!

The primary reason realized that when you start creating a vision board to help you achieve your life purpose, you will feel liberated and no longer believe you must choose between personal and professional fulfillment; you can have BOTH!

Life Purpose Vision Boards liberate you to give and receive in all aspects of your life, including the physical, emotional, intellectual, spiritual, material, creative, adventure, character, financial, and professional aspects.

What Should I Include on My Vision Board for My Life's Purpose?

It is essential to have a crystal-clear mental image of what you request from the universe!

The premise of the Law of purpose is that your predominant thoughts will eventually manifest in your life. From this perspective, you must find a method to align your thoughts with what you wish to do, be, or possess.

Using a specific theme, such as fulfilling your life's purpose, achieving a work-life balance, or manifesting more vitality and prosperity, you can be certain that the items you place on your vision board will support you in making your mark on the world while also helping you to manifest prosperity in every area of your life.

Life Purpose Vision Boards will assist you in manifesting your life's purpose, vision, healing, purposes, destiny, aspirations, desires, wealth, prosperity and abundance, a soulmate, or anything else!

Knowing that thoughts become objects, your dominant thoughts (both subconscious and conscious) manifest in your reality.

Many Helping Professionals feel guilty about placing themselves first or feeling unworthy of receiving payment for their work, even though they know their thoughts determine what they manifest in their lives.

This dominates their thoughts, and this type of negative thinking (poverty thinking) is continuously energized by negative emotion (poverty consciousness); however, because they don't understand how to manifest using the Law of Attraction, they use it in reverse.

Because they are focused on what they don't want, they don't believe they can manifest everything into their reality, they are not genuinely open to receiving, they don't know what they want, or they don't place their attention long enough to manifest anything.

Unfortunately, this is why so many Helping Professionals have had negative experiences with the Law of Attraction and Vision Boards: they don't know how to make them work.

Put into action a plan to align your life's purpose, current business, authentic self, and personal life, and you will start to observe significant changes quickly.

Instead of figuring out or forcing your way to manifest a better existence, you will have a clear mental image and affirm, "I can manifest anything, and it will happen for me.

And soon, you'll be able to manifest your vision for prosperity and abundance using your Life Purpose Vision Board while doing the work you adore!

CHAPTER 15: PURSUING YOUR PURPOSE.

Every morning, we hurry to work, school, and drop off the children and any other busy, hectic errand that eventually ties into the time that eludes us even to be satisfied with our accomplishments. It took me some time to comprehend living in the present moment and how our beliefs shape our actions.

Our generation is divided by the definitions of social class, economic status, academic achievements, and the constant barrage of advertisements attempting to sell us something.

The mind is preoccupied with the conformity of ideologies and philosophies in their relationship to us. We find meaning in the voyage to comprehend what our world signifies and how our egos and selves relate to the interconnectedness of ourselves and the universe.

The human experience is the everyday awareness of how we relate to and respond to environmental stimuli. The physical laws of our planet govern our existence. The flow is effortless, but we need help with culture, social groups, and other divisions in the world.

The Sun rises east of our celestial equator and effortlessly travels across the sky. The purpose is to be able to contribute to the natural laws of our universe using the niche that each of us possesses from birth.

I can attest that most recent graduates who pursue employment encounter a return policy contradiction. Huge loans are granted with the expectation that they will be repaid with principal and interest. The revolving cycle is the hamster on its wheel revolving to catch up to the wheel's final position.

Constant pointing of fingers and apportionment of responsibility never resolve a problem arising from avoidable circumstances but rather keep the mind occupied with matters detrimental to its development.

The desire to influence any subject can only disrupt the universe's natural order.

Most of the time, when a person or entity desires power, more harm is caused in the process. Laws are essential in areas where they don't violate the human rights of any individual; after all, democracy means "for the people, by the people." We are all born free and equal from our mothers' wombs. Respect and dignity are shared purposes.

The mind is a tool unto itself; therefore, it is essential to relay potential outcomes back and forth until it produces a sensation that will benefit you and the person with whom you engage in discussions or conversations.

To place it in a perspective that could shake our mental foundations. We all reside on a small blue asteroid that rotates on its axis relative to the moon, which controls the ocean tides. Every day, the celestial bodies respect one another without any disagreements. We prefer to emphasize our differences to continue constructing the race in which we are all engaged.

What is your purpose? Many distractions include debt, employment, relationships, and the endless destruction of our physical environments. The greater our possessions, the less we gain.

There is an app for every aspect of our lives. We are raising generations of technological machines that must comprehend the limitations necessary to sustain our landscape. We hurry home to avoid human interaction to stare at a lifeless electronic screen depicting recreations of destructive activities and functions.

Accepting the images we see daily on our favorite television programs, films, and other reenactments of stupidity leads to the development of violence. Now, opinions subject us all to the feedback of receiving the information or message to assist in evaluating the results and determining their compatibility with the vibrations of how the world should function.

CONCLUSION.

Living a purposeful existence guides your compass toward achieving your life's purpose. Webster's Dictionary defines Dharma as an individual's duty fulfilled by observance of custom or Law, the fundamental principles of cosmic or individual existence, and conformity to one's duty and nature when following one's intended path.

Your Dharma is the purpose for which you were born. It's what your DNA has programmed you to be and the path of life that will bring you the most pleasure, success, and fulfillment while allowing you to have the greatest impact on humanity. Dharma is comparable to putting on a pair of comfortable slippers. You enjoy wearing them because they suit you so well.

When you are outside Dharma and off your intended path, it is as if you are donning shoes that are too tight, restricting, and uncomfortable; you feel miserable.

When you are in Dharma, all your talents and energy emerge and converge to generate positive results for you and everyone else. You can't help but emanate passion, tranquility, happiness, and fulfillment. Consequently, you will naturally practice fortitude, honesty, compassion, self-control, forgiveness, and logic.

Similarly, living according to your Dharma will assist you in letting go of unwarranted wrath, resentment, judgment, envy, greed, and jealousy. Everyone around you benefits from your Dharma, including yourself. At times, it may appear that you are going against what others want you to do, but if you are in and true to your Dharma.

You are genuinely producing what is best for everyone, including yourself.

Many individuals spend their entire lives outside Dharma or on their intended path. There is no delight whatsoever in this. To live the finest life you're capable of living, you must know who you are and where you're going. As a result, your decisions become much clearer. Consider for a moment whether your dharma shoes are comfortable and properly sized or whether they are too tight or too unfastened.

This book is part of an ongoing collection called "Laws of the Universe."

- ➢ Laws of Assumption.
- ➢ Law of Vibration
- ➢ Law of Polarity
- ➢ Law of Cause & Effect
- ➢ Law of Compensation
- ➢ Law of Correspondence
- ➢ Law of Divine Oneness
- ➢ Law of Rhythm
- ➢ Law of Perpetual Transmutation of Energy
- ➢ Law of Relativity
- ➢ Law of Inspiration
- ➢ Law of Gender and Gestation
- ➢ Law of Reciprocity
- ➢ Law of Purpose
- ➢ Law of Infinite Possibility
- ➢ Law of Unwavering Faith
- ➢ Law of Constant Motion
- ➢ Law of Analogy
- ➢ Law of Free Will
- ➢ Law of Expectation/Expectancy
- ➢ Law of Increase
- ➢ Law of Forgiveness
- ➢ Law of Sacrifice

- Law of Obedience
- Law of Non-Resistance
- Law of Action
- Law of Aspiration to a Higher Power
- Law of Charity
- Law of Compassion
- Law of Courage
- Law of Dedication
- Law of Faith
- Law of Generosity
- Law of Grace
- Law of Honesty
- Law of Hope
- Law of Job
- Law of Kindness
- Law of Leadership
- Law of Non-interference
- Law of Patience
- Law of Praise
- Law of Responsibility
- Law of Self Love
- Law of Thankfulness
- Law of Unconditional Love
- Law of Gravity
- Law of Attraction.

Other Series by Sherry Lee

"Spiritual Attraction."

- ➢ Ask, Believe, Receive.
- ➢ Faith Like a Mustard Seed.
- ➢ You Were Made for Such a Time as This.
- ➢ Let Go and Just Let God Handle it for You.
- ➢ You Have Not Because You Ask Not.
- ➢ Not my Will Lord but Let Your Will be Done.
- ➢ Asking for This or Something Better.
- ➢ What is your Why.
- ➢ God said 365 Times in the Bible; DO NOT BE AFRAID.
- ➢ 10, 100, and 1,000 Fold Increase.
- ➢ Immeasurable More than I Can Hope or Imagine.
- ➢ All Things are Possible, If you Believe.

"Opening and Balancing Your Chakra's"

- ➢ Unblocking your 3rd Eye
- ➢ Opening and Balancing your Heart Chakra
- ➢ Opening and Balancing your Crown Chakra
- ➢ Opening and Balancing your Throat Chakra
- ➢ Opening and Balancing your Solar Plexus Chakra

- ➢ Opening and Balancing your Sacral Chakra
- ➢ Opening and Balancing your Root Chakra.

"Why Alternative Medicine Works"

- ➢ Why Yoga Works
- ➢ Why Chakra Works
- ➢ Why Massage Therapy Works
- ➢ Why Reflexology Works
- ➢ Why Acupuncture Works
- ➢ Why Reiki Works
- ➢ Why Meditation Works
- ➢ Why Hypnosis Works
- ➢ Why Colon Cleansing Works
- ➢ Why NLP (Neuro Linguistic Programming) Works
- ➢ Why Energy Healing Works
- ➢ Why Foot Detoxing Works
- ➢ Why Singing Bowls Works.
- ➢ Why Tapping Works
- ➢ Why Muscle Testing Works.

"Using Sage and Smudging"

- ➢ Learning About Sage and Smudging

- ➤ Sage and Smudging for Love
- ➤ Sage and Smudging for Health and Healing
- ➤ Sage and Smudging for Wealth and Abundance
- ➤ Sage and Smudging for Spiritual Cleansing
- ➤ Sage and Smudging for Negativity.

"Learning About Crystals"

- ➤ Crystals for Love
- ➤ Crystals for Health
- ➤ Crystals for Wealth
- ➤ Crystals for Spiritual Cleansing
- ➤ Crystals for Removing Negativity.

"What Every Newlywed Should Know and Discuss Before Marriage."

- ➤ Newlywed Communication on Money
- ➤ Newlywed Communication on In-laws
- ➤ Newlywed Communication about Children.
- ➤ Newlywed Communication on Religion.
- ➤ Newlywed Communication on Friends.
- ➤ Newlywed Communication on Retirement.
- ➤ Newlywed Communication on Sex.
- ➤ Newlywed Communication on Boundaries.

- ➢ Newlywed Communication on Roles and Responsibilities.

"Health is Wealth."

- ➢ Health is Wealth
- ➢ Positivity is Wealth
- ➢ Emotions is Wealth.
- ➢ Social Health is Wealth.
- ➢ Happiness is Wealth.
- ➢ Fitness is Wealth.
- ➢ Meditating is Wealth.
- ➢ Communication is Wealth.
- ➢ Mental Health is Wealth.
- ➢ Gratitude is Wealth.

"Personal Development Collection."

- ➢ Manifesting for Beginners
- ➢ Crystals for Beginners
- ➢ How to Manifest More Money into Your Life.
- ➢ How to work from home more effectively.
- ➢ How to Accomplish More in Less Time.
- ➢ How to End Procrastination.
- ➢ Learning to Praise and acknowledge your Accomplishments.
- ➢ How to Become Your Own Driving Force.

- Creating a Confident Persona.
- How to Meditate.
- How to Set Affirmations.
- How to Set and Achieve Your Goals.
- Achieving Your Fitness Goals.
- Achieving Your Weight Loss Goals.
- How to Create an Effective Vision Board.

Other Books By Sherry Lee:

- Repeating Angel Numbers
- Most Popular Archangels.
- Askffirmation & Afformations
- Collapsing Time for Supernatural Manifestation.

Author Bio

Sherry Lee. Sherry enjoys reading personal development books, so she decided to write about something she is passionate about. More books will come in this collection, so follow her on Amazon for more books.

Thank you for your purchase of this book.

I honestly do appreciate it and appreciate you, my excellent customer.

God Bless You.

Sherry Lee.